T0353850

Really Sick Jokes

Facing Health Issues with Humor and Grace

Balboa Press books may be ordered through booksellers or by contacting:

Balboa Press
A Division of Hay House
1663 Liberty Drive
Bloomington, IN 47403
www.balboapress.com
844-682-1282

Interior Image Credit: Cathy Pfeil

ISBN: 979-8-7652-5268-0 (sc)
979-8-7652-5269-7 (e)

Library of Congress Control Number: 2024915104

Print information available on the last page.

Balboa Press rev. date: 12/06/2024

BALBOA.PRESS
A DIVISION OF HAY HOUSE

Really Sick Jokes

by Cathy Pfeil

Facing Health Issues with Humor and Grace

iii

Welcome to my world

I have been sick for many years; each year has its ups and downs. I have too much experience having medical procedures and surgeries. I created this little book hoping I can lighten your day with some Really Sick cartoons, some gentle words for healing and some sage advice.

Many of us have events marked by physical trauma or pain. It is easy to fall into a pattern of reliving and grieving one or more of these events even if they happened years ago. These replays can cause us harm physically and emotionally and can leave us expecting another bad outcome. I believe we can learn to shift our perspective and look at our situation in a new, improved way. We are our most powerful when in the present moment.

Lady of I.V's

My journey into healing began when a car going over one hundred miles an hour slammed into our car. I have spent years dealing with a myriad of medical complications, procedures and way too many surgeries. At the beginning I saw myself as a martyr, our lady of the I.V. Since then I have found my center and released my martyrdom.

On the night of the crash, I had a near death experience and began to have visits from people I loved and spiritual teachers. This opened me up to new insights and I continue to learn and grow even now. New insights and perspectives are available to you as well. You do not have to wait for a big crash or other traumatic event to begin a deep spiritual journey.

Dreaming of my Mother

I recommend you find periods of peace and quiet each day to allow space for new insights. I have always journaled and drawn as part of my spiritual journey and to provide a space for these insights.

In the beginning many of my cartoons focused on pain and feeling sorry for myself. Here is the 'migraine angel' who came to visit me often. Instead of dreading the visit I began to look for the first signs of this unwelcome guest. I learned to slow down and listen for what my body needs.

I often balance several medical issues at once and can do very well until a loud noise, fast movement or exhaustion brings things crashing down. This can lead to muscle spasms and panic attacks.

(EASILY STARTLED)

The spasms usually start at my toes and radiate throughout my body often ending in a dislocated jaw. I look for ways to make the tiniest changes as the cramping begins in order to reduce or shorten the episodes. The comfort of family and my service dog make a big difference.

I deal with many medical issues I would never have imagined. Each new issue and resulting medical procedures can seem overwhelming and complicated. If you find yourself with bags, tubes, medical equipment, medication and procedures, it can help to: learn a lot about what is going on, find a support group, talk to people knowledgeable about the issue and take some time figuring out what products and processes work best for you.

Things always seem more complicated at the beginning.

I am always looking for humor in whatever the most recent trauma is. It often takes me some time to find the humor in challenging situations.

On my path, in style

I have found what is still beautiful about me and strive to live my life to the fullest. It was over a year before I could find anything funny about buying diapers.

What to do if you have an accident while out at dinner? Get your food to go, discretely tell your waiter, hold your head high and leave a big tip.

Your family and friends want to help you get well. When asked, I explain all the things I have tried; it is a very long list. But alas, there is always a new thing I have not tried, like a purple drink or a magic crystal or a poke with a sharp stick. If I had just taken this pill or seen this person I would be cured. People will all give you advice, but we must choose our own path. Do what feels right, not only for your physical health but for your emotional health. I suggest sharing strategies only with those who support you.

Brain fog or just general wackiness, my memory is no longer as sharp as it was. I don't recognize my clothes. It started with a bra I found in the wash: my size, brand, and style, but no way was this my bra. I threw it away, along with a box of other clothes someone must have put in my closet. It must be clothes-heimers.

No matter how bad I feel, shopping for art supplies helps. Note my jaunty squirrel cover for my catheter leg bag. No animals were injured in the making of this cartoon!

At the beginning of my recovery, even with all the great care I was receiving, I knew art was to play a significant role in my healing. I began to draw mandalas as my daily meditation.

I have drawn thousands of mandalas. The circle begins, then something wants to be expressed and I follow. They are hand drawn. It is just time, deep breaths and listening to guidance that create my mandalas. My healing lies between the lines, in the direction I receive. Drawing polishes my medical stories like stones in the river, removing the hard edges, revealing what there is to see on a deeper level.

CPfeil. 2018

I thought about getting my final wishes tattooed so there would be no mistake at a critical juncture.

The Tattoo Became Very Complicated:

DO NOT RESUSITATE / DO NOT INTUBATE

No! I changed my mind
DO EVERYTHING UNLESS I AM CHOKING OR AFRAID

No. Just let me go
DNR/DNI FOR SURE

Okay, what if I say
DNR/DNI UNLESS I CHANGE MY MIND OR MY FAMILY
IS SAD THEN DO EVERYTHING YOU CAN

DNR/DNI FOR SURE

...but really I don't want to go
PLEASE LET ME GO IF IT GETS TOO HARD

So it's settled then.
DNR/DNI BUT DO EVERYTHING YOU CAN

Whether a little sniffle or really big sickness, know you can find peace. Figure out what works for you and be grateful for the small things.

I cannot tell you what life looks like without my condition, but I can tell you who I have become.

I am Scar Clan, Lady of Body Metaphor, Night Writer, Shapeshifter.

In this moment take a deep breath. I figure your "spiritual practice" whatever that may be, has prepared you for this moment. Be well, let life come at you in its full glory and deal with what is in front of you. You are surrounded with love, just get ready to once again crawl up out of the ditch and find what works for you.

A few tips for being sick:

Hygiene Take care of yourself physically... brush your teeth, shower, wear clean clothes.

Stay in Touch Call family and friends on a regular basis and remind them to call you too. Don't spend your visit talking about medical issues, yours or theirs.

Physical Touch Whether a pet, a partner or a massage therapist, include non-medical touching in your recovery plan.

Eat What Works for Your Body If someone offers to cook for you take them up on it, but give instructions. Too many tuna cassaroles are not helpful and fast food does not promote healing.

Say YES to Help If someone offers to help (more than a meal), say YES. Have a chore list they can choose from. Ask them to do a load of laundry, clean out the refridgerator, take the dog for a walk. Learning how to receive is a really important part of healing.

Connect —Find a spiritual community, join a study group, meditate with friends or join a book club. Something not related to illness. Discover what is available on-line if you can't get out.

I have enjoyed sharing some of my healing process with you. If I have stirred your interest, there are teachers and healers ready to help you. Check out a book or listen to a podcast to support you. Get a journal and write down your stories. I find people need to tell their Really Sick story until there is no emotion in the telling. I am still working on that part. The key is to not give up.

I hope you have enjoyed my drawings. I have to stop telling stories now to empty my catheter bag.

One day you will tell your story of how you overcame what you went through and it will become someone else's survival guide.

Brene Brown

About the Book

In 1988 my family and I were involved in a head-on car crash. I survived the first night thanks to two surgical teams working simultaneously. This was followed by repeated surgeries and rehab and has left me with serious and lifelong medical complications which require daily attention. It also resulted in a neurological disease which has had a serious impact on my autonomic nervous system.

My healing path has included a myriad of doctors and alternative treatments however none have been more important than my art, humor and positive outlook. Dealing with ongoing medical issues and pain can be a lonely and demoralizing experience. I have worked hard to shift my perspective, find grace in difficult times and see the humor in medical issues and mishaps.

I participate in a number of websites and Social Media for people dealing with similar medical issues. Over the years I have shared my perspective, advice and humor with thousands of people coping with illness.

Really Sick Jokes is an easy and lighthearted read for anyone dealing with medical issues. It encourages readers to shift their perspective on illness and see the humor in challenging situations. The book also shares insights and advice I have used to navigate the journey of healing.

Printed in the United States
by Baker & Taylor Publisher Services